my *Ohio* garden

a gardener's journal

this is my

Ohio

garden

_____

name

_____

year

why keep a garden journal ?

Welcome! We busy Ohio gardeners are often seeking a high-perfor-
mance, low-maintenance landscape. But we take pride in our gardens
and know that gardening is a constant learning process. That's why you
will enjoy *My Ohio Garden: A Gardener's Journal.*

Keeping a garden journal will help you keep track of how your
garden grows. You will discover which plants thrive, which ones
struggle, and best of all, you will discover many surprises. More than
just record keeping, journaling is a way to trace your growth as a
gardener. Writing down your favorite moments in the garden may help
you decide which plants to add or which to replace. How does your
garden make you feel? You may discover you prefer one season to
another. Maybe your style of gardening has changed. A journal will
help you track the evolution in your garden.

As gardeners know, weather is a huge factor in plant performance.
By keeping track of air temperature, the amount of rainfall, and drastic
changes (storms or droughts), we can see which plants survived and
plan better for next year.

Has the environment in your garden changed? Trees and shrubs
that were once small may have matured and created a shadier garden.
Keeping a list of what you plant, where and when you plant it, and the
source of the plant will provide useful information for the future.

Further, keeping up with what's blooming when, and how long it
blooms is another reason to write daily or weekly in a garden journal.
You might be surprised at how many seasons your garden features
beautiful blooms, colorful foliage, or fantastic fruits. Some of the best
color combinations happen by accident and remembering which plant
blooms and when it blooms from year to year is not easy. With good
journal records, you may recreate pleasing plant combinations and
avoid repeating mistakes.

How often you fertilize, prune, and water are other things to keep
track of in your garden journal. Which techniques have been most
successful? If you have a particular pest or disease problem with one
plant, what methods were effective in eradicating or controlling the

problem? If your roses were beautiful last year, when did you prune them and how much did you prune? When did you divide your phlox and where did you plant the different varieties of spring bulbs? All of these questions can be answered in the pages of *My Ohio Garden*.

getting started with your garden journal

By keeping daily records, you can check your journal and chart your most successful garden practices. Whether it's how and when you planted a favorite hydrangea or rose, when the first iris came into bloom, or when you noticed the scent of a particular viburnum, your Ohio garden journal will provide the ideal format for keeping in touch with your garden and what it can teach you. Here's how to begin.

- Designate a day and a time during the week to write in your journal. You might discover that early morning coffee time or the end of the day works best.

- Use a favorite pen and keep it with your journal. Write brief, clear notes (*rainy and cool with temp around 60° F, Phlox 'David' has been in bloom for 2 weeks, Butterfly Bush loaded with flower buds, planted two daylilies in perennial garden*).

- Keep a 5" x 7" envelope tucked in the back of your journal to hold photographs and pictures from catalogs or magazines that inspire you. Be sure to identify and label pictures.

- List existing trees, shrubs, perennials, and bulbs, including a sketch of where they are located. This will be especially helpful over the years when you make changes in your garden.

Once you get used to journaling, you may find that you look forward to writing about your garden as much as you enjoy adding new plants.

Many of us buy plants that strike our eyes, giving no consideration to the location in which we plan to plant them. Canadian hemlock and rhododendron, for example, need special growing conditions to thrive. Roses often wind up in too much shade because we have convinced ourselves that two hours of sun are as good as five.

The USDA cold-hardiness zone map will help you understand your growing environment. A cold-hardiness zone is defined by the northernmost boundary in which plants can grow when the weather is at its coldest. Ohio is divided into two cold-hardiness zones, 5 and 6.

Study the environmental conditions in your garden and let the garden tell you what to do. Familiarize yourself with the native or common plants of your region and use them as a guide to selections for your garden, both native and exotic. Knowing the type of soil, light, and exposure your plants require will help you select the right plant for the right place. You will probably want to select plants that tolerate your landscape's climate to increase survival and minimize maintenance. With the exception of large trees and shrubs, don't be afraid to move your plants. The best time of year to do this is early spring, before the new growth appears. Often conditions change, and what was once a favorable environment may no longer be. Proper watering, mulch, and fertilizer further help to ensure the success of your garden.

the plan

It can be useful to consult a professional landscape designer or architect to help you plan your garden. Their work can be as detailed as a drawing with every plant sited or as broad as a simple list of recommended plants for particular areas. If you have just moved into your house, observe the garden one whole growing season before you hire someone to help you develop a plan. This experience will help you determine which areas receive the most light and which are in shade, etc. Once you have a plan, you can implement it in stages over time. Making adjustments as conditions or your tastes change is easy. You may also refer to my book, *The Gardening Book for Ohio* (Cool Springs Press, 2000), for specific plant recommendations and advice for Ohio gardeners.

soil

Good soil is essential for a fruitful garden and is the foundation of our landscape. There are parts of northern Ohio that have very good soil, while other parts of northern Ohio have sandy soil. There is some good soil in southern and eastern Ohio, but most of us have clay soil in various thicknesses.

Soil is composed of mineral material, organic matter, water, and air. The mineral matter comes from the weathering of bedrock, which combines with organic matter from dead plants, manure, and other decomposing materials. It is important to know what type of soil you have in order to garden successfully.

amending your soil

For years, it was standard practice to tell homeowners installing new plants to amend the soil and to add peat moss, compost, manure, and all the above to the soil you dug out while digging the hole. Common sense is now convincing the industry to tell you that it is possible to overamend your soil. What kind of soil is the plant going to grow in once the roots grow beyond the hole you dug? Overimproving the existing soil, or worse, yet, replacing the old soil with fresh topsoil creates what I call "bathtubbing". When it rains or when we water, the moisture goes through the overamended soil very quickly, hitting the hard clay bottom and filling up like a bathtub. Too much water equals a dead plant.

I recommend using organic peat or pine bark chips to amend soil when needed, but do not add more than 30% amendments to mix with the existing soil. Always break up your clay soil so no particle is bigger than a golf ball. Compost is one of the best soil amendments available because it is alive with billions of creatures that help roots absorb water and nutrients. Composting can be as simple as piling leaves and clippings in a heap and letting them break down. You can add kitchen waste such as coffee grounds, clean eggshells, and uncooked vegetable scraps to your compost pile. It is best not to add animal fats, bones, or meat. Be patient! It will take approximately six months and a 30-gallon bag of yard trimmings to yield 1 cubic foot of compost from your pile.

watering

Watering seems like a simple thing, but gardeners have a tendency to overwater or underwater plants. Sandy soils drain quickly, requiring watering often during blistering summers. Clay soils hold water, therefore plants growing in clay need less watering. Don't water by a schedule. Always check the soil with a garden trowel, digging down 4-5 inches, to see if moisture is needed.

guidelines for watering:

- Water your container plants until the water runs out the bottom. During hot summer months some containers may need water twice a day. Do not water until the top inch of the soil is dry to the touch.
- Put a hose at the base of a newly installed tree or shrub and thoroughly soak the rootball when it's dry. As the plant grows, the area that needs to be soaked will increase as the root zone increases.

- Use shallow cans (tuna, etc.) to measure the amount of water applied by your lawn sprinkler. Put six cans in the area you are watering and run the system for an hour. Then measure the depth of the water in all cans. When the average depth of the water is 1 inch, the grass root zone has been irrigated. This may take one to four hours.
- Buy an inexpensive water timer and a few soaker hoses. They are a worthwhile investment. During periods of drought mature trees will benefit from long, slow watering.

mulch

Mulch discourages weeds and retains moisture. It acts like a blanket, holding moisture in the soil and keeping the soil temperature from getting too hot or cold. Mulch can also help reduce weed infestations. But use common sense! Too much can prevent air and water from getting to the plant's roots. Some plants mulch themselves with their own foliage spread.

tips when mulching:
- Apply a 1- to 2-inch layer of mulch on top of the soil around all plants. At the same time, avoid piling mulch against the trunks or stems of plants. This could lead to potential disease problems.
- Hardwood chips, shredded leaves, and compost are good choices.

nutrients

The main nutrients plants need are nitrogen, phosphorous, and potassium. When you buy fertilizer you will see three numbers on the bag representing the percentage by weight of each nutrient in the mixture. For example, a bag of 10-10-10 fertilizer contains 10%

nitrogen (N), 10% phosphorus (P), and 10% potassium (K). The other 70% is an inert filler.

Each nutrient serves a function in the overall good health of a plant. Nitrogen promotes leaf growth. That is why lawn fertilizer has a high nitrogen percentage. Phosphorous is important in the formation of roots, as well as flower, seed, and fruit growth. That is why starter fertilizers and bloom fertilizers have high percentages of phosphorous. Potassium increases overall cell health. When plants are under stress from drought or cold, adequate potassium helps them withstand the crisis.

soil test

A soil test helps determine how much fertilizer to apply and whether any additives (such as lime) are needed. The Ohio Extension Service can provide you with the necessary forms and information for soil testing, or you can contact a state-certified, soil-testing laboratory. Soil acidity is measured in numbers from 1 to 14 on the pH scale, where 7 is neutral. Most plants prefer a soil that has a pH of 6.0 to 6.5. The soil test report will tell you how much and what type of fertilizer or other additives to use for the type of plant you are growing, the soil pH and what, if anything, should be done to protect it.

get started journaling and have fun

Your garden is what you make it. If you keep your heart and mind open to the nuances of nature, you will cultivate more than just pretty flowers and strong trees. Both you and your plants will grow in your beautiful garden. Hopefully, you will also have fun creating lovely gardens. HAPPY GARDENING!

Ohio Garden Favorites

I selected a list of plants that are easy to grow, readily available, adaptable to various growing conditions, and help provide year-round interest. These plants can be very beneficial to your Ohio garden because they provide brilliant color, some attract birds and wildlife, and most require minimal maintenance. You will find most of my recommendations in my book *The Gardening Book for Ohio* (Cool Springs Press, 2000). Give these a try!

Annuals

- Scaevola — *Scaevola aemula*
- Vinca — *Catharanthus roseus*
- Impatiens — *Impatiens wallerana*
- Melampodium — *Melampodium paludosum*
- Million Bells® — *Calibrachoa* hybrids
- Petunias — *Petunia* x *hybrida*
- Blue Salvia — *Salvia farinacea*
- Wax-Leaf Begonia — *Begonia* hybrids
- Pentas — *Pentas lanceolata*
- Torenia — *Torenia fournieri*

Perennials

- Daylily — *Homerocallis* hybrids
- Pincushion Flower — *Scabiosa caucasica* 'Fama'
- Hosta — *Hosta* spp. and hybrids
- Black-Eyed Susan — *Rudbeckia fulgida* var. *sullivantii* 'Goldsturm' —
- Stokes' Asters — *Stokesia laevis*
- Coreopsis — *Coreopsis verticillata* 'Moonbeam'
- Garden Mum — *Chrysanthemum* x *morifolium*
- Gayfeather — *Liatris spicata*
- Astilbe — *Astilbe* x *arendsii*
- Coneflower — *Echinacea purpurea*

Bulbs

- Daffodil — *Narcissus* species and cultivars
- Caladium — *Caladium* x *hortulanum*
- Allium — *Allium* spp.
- Crocus — *Crocus vernus*
- Dahlia — *Dahlia* hybrids
- Tulips — *Tulipa* cultivars
- Scilla — *Scilla siberica*
- Grape Hyacinth — *Muscari* spp.
- Tuberous Begonia — *Begonia* x *tuberhybrida*
- Canna — *Canna* x *generalis*

Vines

- Clematis — *Clematis* hybrids
- Climbing Hydrangea — *Hydrangea anomala* spp. *petiolaris*
- Virginia Creeper — *Parthenocissus quinquefolia*
- Mandevilla — *Mandevilla* x *amabilis*
- Boston Ivy — *Parthenocissus tricuspidata*
- Trumpet Vine — *Campsis radicans*
- Silver Lace Vine — *Polygonum aubertii*
- Wisteria — *Wisteria floribunda*
- Moonflower — *Ipomoea alba*
- Morning Glory — *Ipomoea purpurea*

Turfgrasses

- Turf-type Tall Fescue — *Festuca* cultivars
- Kentucky Blue Grass — *Poa* cultivars
- Fine-Leaf Fescue — *Festuca* cultivars
- Perennial Rye — *Lolium* cultivars
- Zoysia — *Zoysia* cultivars

Trees

- Flowering Crabapple — *Malus* spp. and cultivars
- Serviceberry — *Amelanchier arborea*
- Ornamental Pear — *Pyrus calleryana*
- Sweet Bay Magnolia — *Magnolia virginiana*
- Norway Spruce — *Picea abies*

- White Ash — *Fraxinus americana*
- Eastern Redbud — *Cercis canadensis*
- Carolina Silver Bell — *Halesia carolina*
- 'Winter King' Hawthorn — *Crataegus virdis* 'Winter King'
- Silver Linden — *Tilia tomentosa*

Shrubs

- Blue Holly — *Ilex x meservaea* hybrids
- Goldencup St. Johnswort — *Hypericum patulum* 'Sungold'
- Korean Boxwood — *Buxus microphylla* var. *koreana*
- Green Emerald Arborvitae — *Thuja occidentalis* 'Smaragd'

- Dwarf Spirea — *Spiraea* x *bumalda*
- Butterfly Bush — *Buddleia davidii*
- Dwarf Burning Bush — *Euonymus alatus* 'Compactus'
- Viburnum 'Alleghany' — *Viburnum* x *rhytidophylloides*
- Bayberry — *Myrica pensylvanica*

Ground covers

- English Ivy — *Hedera helix*
- Wintercreeper — *Euonymus fortunei* 'Coloratus'
- Lily Turf — *Liriope muscar* i
- Ajuga — *Ajuga reptans*
- Pachysandra — *Pachysandra terminalis*

- Myrtle — *Vinca minor*
- Creeping Juniper — *Juniperus* cultivars
- Lily-of-the-Valley — *Convallaria majalis*
- Chameleon Plant — *Houttuynia cordata*
- Creeping Phlox — *Phlox subulata*

Ornamental grasses

- Fountain Grass — *Pennisetum alopecuroides* 'Hameln'
- Maiden Grass — *Miscanthus sinensis* 'Gracillimus'
- Japanese Blood Grass — *Imperata cylindrical* 'Rubra'
- Blue Fescue — *Festuca ovina* 'Glauca'

- Feather Reed Grass — *Calamagrostis x acutiflora* 'Overdam'
- Northern Sea Oats — *Chasmanthium latifolium*
- Ribbon Grass — *Phalaris arundinacea* 'Picta'

Roses

- Hedge Rose — *Rosa* 'Bonica' Meidiland™
- Shrub Rose — *Rosa* 'Care Free Beauty'
- Miniature Rose — *Rosa* 'Lady Sunblaze'

- Climbing Rose — *Rosa* 'Golden Showers'
- Grandiflora Rose — *Rosa* 'Fame'
- Hybrid Tea Rose — *Rosa* 'Show Biz'

Average Annual Minimum Temperature

5A	-15° F to -20° F
5B	-10° F to -15° F
6A	-5° F to -10° F
6B	0° F to -5° F

garden notes

I placed my seed orders, and I ordered some strawberries, as well. Now I'm just waiting for them to arrive!

garden observations

what's the weather like?

Take a walk through
your garden, and
plan additions to
create winter interest
for next year.

Did You Know?
The only tulip color
that has not yet been
developed is any
shade of blue.

what have I planted/transplanted?

garden notes

February

garden observations

_____

_____

_____

_____

_____

_____

_____

what's the weather like?

_____

_____

_____

_____

_____

_____

When in doubt,
call your local
Extension Service.
Master Gardeners
there will provide
information (and
the advice is free!)

what have I planted/transplanted?

_____

_____

_____

_____

_____

_____

_____

garden notes

February

garden observations

Extend the life of
your cut flowers.
Remove the lower
leaves and re-cut the
stems before
arranging them in
lukewarm water.

what's the weather like?

what have I planted/transplanted?

garden notes

Though I do not believe
that a plant will spring
up where no seed has been,
I have great faith in a
seed. Convince me that
you have a seed there,
and I am prepared to
expect wonders.

—Henry David Thoreau

february | week 4

February

garden observations

_____
_____
_____
_____
_____
_____

what's the weather like?

_____
_____
_____
_____
_____
_____

Tip to Remember:
Fill clear plastic
milk jugs with
water and place
around young
tomato plants.
They will provide
warmth overnight
for young plants,
helping you get a
jump on spring.

what have I planted/transplanted?

_____
_____
_____
_____
_____

garden notes

february | week 4

march | week 1

March

what's blooming?

Direct sow wildflower
seeds where you want
them to grow in
climates with USDA
zones 1 through 6.
(Check the zone map
in the introduction to
identify your zone.)

what's the weather like?

Take a soil test now
so you will know how
to prepare your garden
for the next season.

what have I planted/transplanted?

garden notes

march week 2

March

what's blooming?

Tip to Remember:
Plan to add a few
annuals to your
perennial garden
to help provide
season-long blooms.

what's the weather like?

Watch for aphids on
shrubs as they leaf out.
Treat with insecticidal
soap or any other
labeled pesticide,
if needed.

what have I planted/transplanted?

Start tomato seeds for
transplants 4-6 weeks
before optimum plant-
ing time in your area.

garden notes

m a r c h | w e e k 3

March

what's blooming?

Single-flower forms of
marigolds and zinnias
are more appealing to
butterflies than the
double-flower forms.

what's the weather like?

Did You Know?
Viburnum is a
member of the
honeysuckle family.

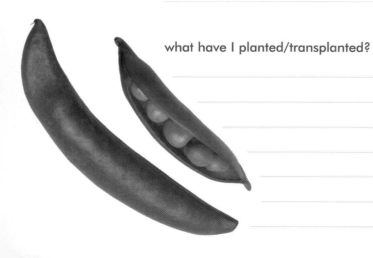

what have I planted/transplanted?

garden notes

what's blooming?

what's the weather like?

Hummingbirds love tubular flowers such as trumpet vine, coral honeysuckle, and nicotiana. Plant lots of these if you want to attract hummingbirds.

what have I planted/transplanted?

garden notes

Half the interest of a garden is the constant exercise of the imagination.

— C.W. Earle

april | week 1

April

what's blooming?

_____
_____
_____
_____
_____

what's the weather like?

_____
_____
_____
_____
_____

Have you photographed your garden lately? This will help with your garden planning and design ideas.

what have I planted/transplanted?

_____
_____
_____
_____
_____

An easy time to weed is the day after a gentle rain, when the soil is slightly moist, and weeds are easy to pull—roots and all.

garden notes

april | week 1

April

Propagate some
of your favorite
broadleaf shrubs using
this simple layering
technique: Select a
branch that is close to
the ground. Bend the
branch so that it is in
contact with the soil.
Cover the branch
with soil. Water well
and hold the branch
in place with a brick.
In six weeks, check to
see if there are roots.
Once the roots are
firmly established,
cut the new plant
off from the
mother plant.

what's blooming?

what's the weather like?

what have I planted/transplanted?

garden notes

As is the gardener, such is the garden.

— Hebrew Proverb

april | week 3

what's blooming?

Tip to Remember:
When digging a hole
for a tree, it's best to
dig the hole at least
half again as wide as
the size of the rootball
(much wider is even
better). Use the same
soil you dug out to
backfill around
the rootball and
water-in well.

what's the weather like?

Turn your compost
pile. If you haven't
started one already,
call your Extension
Service for advice.

what have I planted/transplanted?

garden notes

april | week 4

what's blooming?

what's the weather like?

Wooden clothespins
can be used as plant
markers.

Place grow-thru stakes
above plants that need
support in early
spring, and in a
short time they will
cover the stakes.

what have I planted/transplanted?

garden notes

Plan to prune back spring-blooming azaleas and other shrubs such as forsythia or spirea after they finish flowering. This way you won't cut off any potential flower buds for next year.

Check plants once or twice a week for insect and disease problems. It's easier to control a small infestation if it's discovered early.

what's blooming?

what's the weather like?

what have I planted/transplanted?

garden notes

may week 2

May

what's blooming?

_____

_____

_____

_____

_____

_____

what's the weather like?

_____

_____

_____

_____

_____

_____

Incorporate a
slow-release fertilizer
in the soil of hanging
baskets and container
plantings. This will
provide nutrients for
several months in
one application.

what have I planted/transplanted?

_____

_____

_____

_____

_____

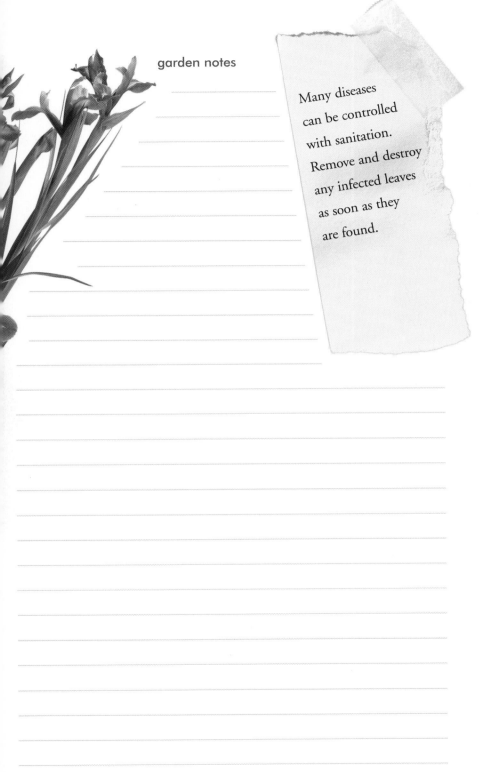

garden notes

Many diseases
can be controlled
with sanitation.
Remove and destroy
any infected leaves
as soon as they
are found.

May

what's blooming?

Parsley and fennel
provide food for
butterfly caterpillars.

what's the weather like?

Interest children
in gardening by
planning a small
child's garden. A
bean tee-pee is fun
to plant and grow!

what have I planted/transplanted?

garden notes

The best time for slug hunting is at night using a flashlight and a pair of gloves.

may week 4

May

what's blooming?

what's the weather like?

what have I planted/transplanted?

garden notes

Tickle it with a hoe and it will laugh into a harvest.

—English Proverb

June

A perennial garden looks wonderful when planted against a background of a wall, a hedge, or evergreen shrubs.

A plant's scientific name consists of a genus and an epithet. The genus and the epithet are always italicized and the genus begins with a capital letter. A third word in the name may refer to a specific variety, called a cultivar. It is set off by single quotation marks.

what's blooming?

what's the weather like?

what have I planted/transplanted?

garden notes

June

what's blooming?

Use vines to create
vertical interest in the
garden. If you don't
have a wall or fence
on which to train
them, a lattice or
arbor will work.

what's the weather like?

You can create
your own portable
seep irrigation
system by punch-
ing a few holes in
plastic containers
and placing them
beside plants that
need additional
moisture.

what have I planted/transplanted?

garden notes

Though an old man, I am but a young gardener...

— Thomas Jefferson

june | week 3

June

Plan to shear fall-blooming asters to make them bushier and more compact.

what's blooming?

what's the weather like?

Did You Know?
Even though a plant may be identified as self-cleaning, flowers are better off if you deadhead, or remove the spent blooms as often as you can. This will allow the plant to use its energy to make more flowers and leaves instead of making seeds.

what have I planted/transplanted?

garden notes

_____
_____
_____
_____
_____
_____
_____
_____
_____
_____
_____
_____
_____
_____
_____
_____
_____
_____
_____

June

what's blooming?

what's the weather like?

BTK (*Bacillus thuringiensis kurstaki*) is an organic biological control that is effective against many caterpillars and is safe to use on vegetable crops. *Bacillus thuringiensis* 'San Diego' is effective against some leafeating beetles.

what have I planted/transplanted?

garden notes

july week 1

July

Harvest herbs for drying as soon as they come into flower. Bundle them up with a rubber band and hang them on a line in a dark, dry place with good air circulation. To preserve the best flavor once they are dry, store the herbs in airtight containers away from heat and light.

Press some flowers and add to this journal. It's a pretty record of what you planted.

what's blooming?

what's the weather like?

what have I planted/transplanted?

garden notes

what's blooming?

Lantana, petunias, cosmos,
Arabian Night dahlia
Echinacea, coreopsis
Rudbeckia, scabiosa,
Salvia, veronica

what's the weather like?

Weather has been hot
and humid with
scattered thunder
showers. We received
2 ½ inches of rain
this week.

Deadhead hybrid tea
roses throughout the
summer to encourage
more blooms.

what have I planted/transplanted?

At this point,
everything for the
summer garden
has been planted
or transplanted.

garden notes

The yellow zucchini are
HUGE!! I planted four.
Two would have been sufficient!

The Rutgers tomatoes are
HEAVY determinates that
would have benefited from
cages. I'm supporting them
with flat bungee cables this
year, but will definitely
cage next year.

Currently harvesting:

Yellow zucchini
Basil

july week 3

what's blooming?

what's the weather like?

Most unwanted
summer heat comes
through east- and west-
facing windows, not
through well-insulated
roofs and walls. Plant a
deciduous tree for shade.

what have I planted/transplanted?

garden notes

july week 4

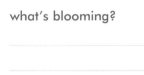

what's blooming?

Plants use calcium to build strong cell walls and stems. Deficiencies can cause blossom-end rot on tomatoes.

what's the weather like?

Did You Know? The Greeks and Romans used lavender in bath water. In fact, the Latin name "lavare" means, "wash".

Tip to Remember: When planting seeds, position them in geometric patterns so that you will be able to distinguish them more easily from weed seedlings.

what have I planted/transplanted?

garden notes

Gardening is the purest of human pleasures.

— Francis Bacon

August

what's blooming?

what's the weather like?

Preserve basil leaves by mixing them in the blender with a small amount of water. Fill ice cube trays with the mixture. Once they freeze, put them in freezer bags. This way you will have basil to use in your favorite Italian dishes all winter long.

what have I planted/transplanted?

garden notes

august | week 1

a u g u s t | week 2

August

what's blooming?

For the best selection, order your spring-flowering bulbs or purchase them locally when they become available in your area. Keep them cool and dry until you plant them.

what's the weather like?

Take some photographs of your garden to refer to later when planning for next year.

what have I planted/transplanted?

garden notes

august | week 2

august week 3

August

If you haven't already done so, draw a plan of your property showing existing trees and shrubs in relation to your house. Make notes throughout the year indicating those areas that receive full sun, shade or a mix of sun and shade. This will help you to choose the right plant for the right place.

what's blooming?

what's the weather like?

what have I planted/transplanted?

august | week 4

August

August

what's blooming?

Water your compost pile when the weather has been dry.

what's the weather like?

Order three or four types of paperwhite narcissus to force at two-week intervals. You will have flowers from Halloween into the New Year!

Continue to harvest vegetables as soon as they are ripe. Regular harvesting increases production.

what have I planted/transplanted?

garden notes

*He who plants
a garden plants
happiness.*
—Chinese Proverb

september | week 1

september

what's blooming?

_____

_____

_____

_____

_____

_____

what's the weather like?

_____

_____

_____

_____

_____

Expand your plant
collection by exchang-
ing seeds and plants
with fellow gardeners.

what have I planted/transplanted?

_____

_____

Add some shrubs to
your garden that will
offer winter interest
such as colorful bark,
or unusual shapes.

_____

_____

_____

_____

garden notes

what's blooming?

what's the weather like?

If you haven't
started one
already, begin
a compost pile
and let it
overwinter.
In six months
you should
have "black
gold" to mix
into your
garden.

what have I planted/transplanted?

garden notes

The frost hurts not weeds.

— Thomas Fuller

september

what's blooming?

_____

_____

_____

_____

_____

_____

what's the weather like?

_____

_____

_____

_____

_____

_____

what have I planted/transplanted?

_____

_____

_____

_____

_____

garden notes

If your annuals are beginning to look ragged, pull them and replace with some mums, pansies, or flowering kale.

september | week 4

september

what's blooming?

Use dried seed
heads such as sedum
and lotus for fall
decorations.

Visit your favorite
nursery to select a tree
or shrub for that spot
in the garden that
needs something new.

what's the weather like?

what have I planted/transplanted?

garden notes

september | week 4

october | week 1

October

what's blooming?

_____

_____

_____

_____

_____

_____

_____

what's the weather like?

Plant a tree in honor
of a birth or in
memory of a
loved one.

_____

_____

_____

_____

Fall leaf color is trig-
gered by cooler tem-
peratures, shorter
days, and less light.

what have I planted/transplanted?

_____

_____

_____

_____

_____

_____

_____

garden notes

October

what's blooming?

what's the weather like?

what have I planted/transplanted?

garden notes

Sprinkle annual
rye grass seed on
top of the soil
of pots you are
forcing. By the
time the bulbs
bloom, it will
create a green carpet
underneath them.

october | week 3

October

what's blooming?

what's the weather like?

Tip to Remember:
Parsley is a good
plant for bed edges.
It also looks great
grown in containers
with pansies.

what have I planted/transplanted?

Use golf tees to mark
areas where bulbs are
planted.

garden notes

*Heaven is under our feet
as well as over our heads.*
— Henry David Thoreau

october | week 4

October

what's blooming?

what's the weather like?

Did You Know?
The word 'wort',
as in St. John's Wort,
is an old English
term that means
"medicinal plant".

what have I planted/transplanted?

garden notes

october | week 4

November

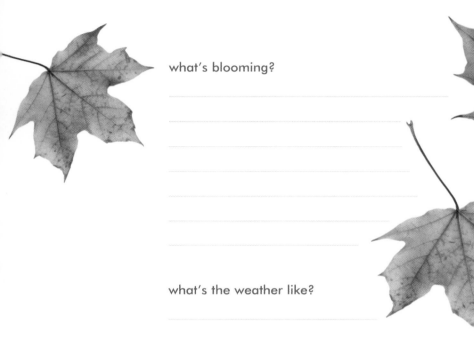

what's blooming?

what's the weather like?

Fall is the best time
to direct sow wild-
flower seeds in
USDA zones 7-9.
(Check the map in
the introduction to
verify your zone.)

what have I planted/transplanted?

garden notes

Autumn is a second spring when every leaf is a flower. —Albert Camus

November

what's blooming?

_____
_____
_____
_____
_____
_____
_____

what's the weather like?

_____
_____
_____
_____
_____
_____

Continue to mow
your lawn for as long
as it keeps growing.

Clean and sharpen
garden tools. Lightly
coat with oil to
prevent rust.

what have I planted/transplanted?

_____
_____
_____
_____
_____
_____

garden notes

November

what's blooming?

_____
_____
_____
_____
_____

what's the weather like?

_____
_____
_____
_____
_____

what have I planted/transplanted?

_____
_____
_____
_____
_____

garden notes

_____
_____
_____
_____
_____
_____
_____

_____
_____
_____
_____
_____
_____
_____
_____

Extend the life of
your fresh-cut holiday
tree by storing it in a
cool shady place until
you move it indoors.
Re-cut the trunk
before moving it
indoors and use
plenty of fresh water
in the reservoir.

_____
_____
_____
_____
_____
_____
_____
_____
_____

november | week 3

November

what's blooming?

For best results, store
unused seeds in a
cool, dark place in
an air- and water-
resistant container.

Selecting the right
tool for the job can
prevent most injuries.
Wear safety gear
when operating
power equipment.

what's the weather like?

what have I planted/transplanted?

garden notes

november | week 4

december | week 1

December

garden observations

_____

_____

_____

_____

_____

_____

Make a wreath for
the holidays. Rose
hips, bittersweet, and
euonymus are good
choices for materials.

what's the weather like?

_____

_____

_____

_____

what have I planted/
transplanted?

_____

_____

_____

_____

garden notes

*A garden is a friend
you can visit any time.*
— unknown

December

garden observations

Cast iron plant, Chinese evergreen, heartleaf philodendron, and snake plant will tolerate low-light conditions.

what's the weather like?

Tip to Remember: The winter sun provides the most solar heat through south-facing windows. Avoid planting shade trees or evergreens that may shade these heat-absorbing windows if you need the extra warmth.

what have I planted/transplanted?

garden notes

december | week 3

December

garden observations

what's the weather like?

what have I planted/transplanted?

Recycle your holiday tree. The branches can be removed and used as mulch. Or you can leave the tree intact and use it as a windbreak and shelter for birds.

Don't put wood ashes in your compost pile; they will alter the pH level too much.

garden notes

December

garden observations

what's the weather like?

what have I planted/transplanted?

garden notes

Pruning large trees, especially those located near utilities should be performed by a professional. Call a certified arborist if you need trees pruned.

plant inventory/history

name	name
when planted	when planted
where planted	where planted
size	size
source	source
price	price

name	name
when planted	when planted
where planted	where planted
size	size
source	source
price	price

name	name
when planted	when planted
where planted	where planted
size	size
source	source
price	price

name	name
when planted	when planted
where planted	where planted
size	size
source	source
price	price

name		name	
when planted		when planted	
where planted		where planted	
size		size	
source		source	
price		price	

name		name	
when planted		when planted	
where planted		where planted	
size		size	
source		source	
price		price	

name		name	
when planted		when planted	
where planted		where planted	
size		size	
source		source	
price		price	

name		name	
when planted		when planted	
where planted		where planted	
size		size	
source		source	
price		price	

plant inventory/history

name

when planted

where planted

size

source

price

name

when planted

where planted

size

source

price

name

when planted

where planted

size

source

price

name

when planted

where planted

size

source

price

name

when planted

where planted

size

source

price

name

when planted

where planted

size

source

price

name

when planted

where planted

size

source

price

name

when planted

where planted

size

source

price

name

when planted

where planted

size

source

price

name

when planted

where planted

size

source

price

name

when planted

where planted

size

source

price

name

when planted

where planted

size

source

price

name

when planted

where planted

size

source

price

name

when planted

where planted

size

source

price

name

when planted

where planted

size

source

price

name

when planted

where planted

size

source

price

plant inventory/history

name	**name**
when planted	when planted
where planted	where planted
size	size
source	source
price	price

name	**name**
when planted	when planted
where planted	where planted
size	size
source	source
price	price

name	**name**
when planted	when planted
where planted	where planted
size	size
source	source
price	price

name	**name**
when planted	when planted
where planted	where planted
size	size
source	source
price	price

name

when planted

where planted

size

source

price

name

when planted

where planted

size

source

price

name

when planted

where planted

size

source

price

name

when planted

where planted

size

source

price

name

when planted

where planted

size

source

price

name

when planted

where planted

size

source

price

name

when planted

where planted

size

source

price

name

when planted

where planted

size

source

price

plant inventory/history

name

when planted

where planted

size

source

price

name

when planted

where planted

size

source

price

name

when planted

where planted

size

source

price

name

when planted

where planted

size

source

price

name

when planted

where planted

size

source

price

name

when planted

where planted

size

source

price

name

when planted

where planted

size

source

price

name

when planted

where planted

size

source

price

name

when planted

where planted

size

source

price

name

when planted

where planted

size

source

price

name

when planted

where planted

size

source

price

name

when planted

where planted

size

source

price

name

when planted

where planted

size

source

price

name

when planted

where planted

size

source

price

name

when planted

where planted

size

source

price

name

when planted

where planted

size

source

price

my garden plan

suppliers & resources

photos